Migration Nation

Migration Nation

Animals on the Go from Coast to Coast

Joanne O'Sullivan

imagine!
Publishing

To Andrew, Maeve, and Finn:
my pod, my pack,
my kaleidoscope,
my aurora, and the
best travel partners
for life's journeys

Image copyrights held by the photographers on page 95.

Text Copyright © 2015 by Joanne O'Sullivan

Ranger Rick and National Wildlife Federation logos and artwork all rights reserved. © 2015 National Wildlife Federation
www.nwf.org
www.nwf.org/rangerrick

An Imagine Book
Published by Charlesbridge
85 Main Street
Watertown, MA 02472
(617) 926-0329
www.charlesbridge.com

Library of Congress Cataloging-in-Publication Data
is available upon request.

ISBN: 978-1-62354-050-0

Printed in China. Manufactured January, 2015.

(hc) 10 9 8 7 6 5 4 3 2 1

Display type and text type set in Badger and Univers
Interior design: Megan Kirby
Produced by EarlyLight Books

For information about custom editions, special sales, premium and corporate purchases, please contact Charlesbridge Publishing at specialsales@charlesbridge.com

CONTENTS

INTRODUCTION

Ready to go on a journey? It's a wild trip through rushing rivers, across frozen ice floes, and through stormy skies. It will take you from Mexico across the Great Plains, through Pacific waters, and as far north as the Arctic Circle. Your travel companions are some of North America's most interesting animals.

Why Migrate?

Migration is the seasonal movement of wildlife from one place to another for food or breeding. Animals migrate for survival, not fun. Their lives revolve around the seasons and the environment. In fall, animals migrate south, where food is still abundant. In spring, they migrate north, where food is once again becoming available so they can reproduce. Animals don't use calendars or information in books to tell them when to migrate. Instead, the amount of daylight and temperatures triggers their migration instinct.

Migration Routes

Migration isn't easy! The monarch butterfly starts its spring migration in Mexico, and the polar bear moves from the far north of the Arctic Circle into the Hudson Bay area of Canada. These two animals are as different as they can be, but the same environmental issues have a big impact on both. You'll read about the roadblocks they face along the way and about the ways that people are trying to help them. You'll discover ways that you can help them, too!

Animal road trips do not necessarily follow roads. Migration paths can be invisible to humans. Animals know the paths through chemical, magnetic, or temperature cues that we haven't quite figured out yet.

Travel Along . . .

In this book, you'll follow the paths of twelve very different types of animals, exploring how and why they take their road trips. You'll learn about the animals' versions of road food (hint: they don't have drive-thrus) and how they stay fueled up for their journeys, long or short. You'll also find out what's unique about each of these migrators.

Animals are on the go! Hold onto your seat and come along for the ride on these wild road trips.

Migration by LAND

Imagine an invisible superhighway for animals. It has no borders and no painted lines. It has no rules and no speed limit. Humans can't see it, but animals know exactly where to go. Each year, twice a year, these invisible roads are busy with traffic from hooves, pads, paws, wings, and bellies as animals travel to and from their seasonal homes.

Snakes may not have feet, but that doesn't mean they can't take to the roads, slithering on their bellies from their winter dens to summer homes and back again. Pronghorns streak down their migration path on legs selected for speed. American bison trek from higher to lower elevations. Polar bears are not known for traveling long distances, but their migration is one of the world's most amazing journeys!

Pack your bags and start turning pages!

SNAKE ROAD: Along the Herptile Highway

On a wet, moonless night in early May, the herptiles are stirring. (Herptile is a nickname biologists use to describe reptiles and amphibians together.) The woodland's toads, frogs, newts, and salamanders are shaking off their winter sleep. Although some newts and many frogs and salamanders overwinter at the bottom of ponds, others spend the winter in burrows. The rising temperatures set off their internal alarm clocks. It's dark; it's warmer; it's wet: it's time to get going! Those that spend their winters in burrows hop, crawl, and slink out to start their journeys. They can smell water, and they move toward it at a still-sleepy pace.

High up in the rocky bluffs, snakes are starting to slither downward. Now that they are awake, they're getting hungry. Some species need to get to the water, where they can hide from predators and sneak up on prey animals.

On what's called the big night, these herptiles are all headed in the same direction—toward the swamp. But they've got to cross a road to get there. Not just any road: they are heading into rush-hour traffic on Snake Road.

PLEASE BRAKE FOR SNAKES . . . AND TURTLES AND TOADS

LaRue Swamp (below) is on one side. The tall bluffs along the Mississippi River are on the other. Snake Road runs in between the swamp and the bluffs, in the Shawnee National Forest in southern Illinois. For a few months each spring and fall, Snake Road is herptile central.

During each migration season, Snake Road is closed to anything with wheels. In fact, Snake Road is said to be the *only* road in the United States that shuts down for snake migration. That's because fast-moving vehicles and slow-moving snakes, turtles, toads, and salamanders are a bad mix. Now that the herptiles are protected, there are dozens of snakes and *hundreds* of amphibians on peak migration days and nights. Can you imagine what that would look like? It's a creepy, crawly free-for-all!

LEFT: LaRue Swamp in Shawnee National Forest in southern Illinois

THE MIGRATION PATH

LaRue Pine Hills
Shawnee National Forest

Snake
Road

QUICK FACTS

FROM: Winter dens in
Shawnee National Forest

TO: Summer home near rivers and ponds

MILES TRAVELED: From ¼ mile to 5 miles

SEASONS TRAVELED: Spring and fall

WHY DID THE TOAD CROSS THE ROAD?

The herptile migration at Shawnee is one of the biggest and best, but amphibians everywhere migrate in much the same way. Conditions need to be just right—the temperature must rise into the mid 40s° F. It should be raining or have recently rained. The sky should be dark—no moon or shining stars. When all these conditions are in place, toads, salamanders, newts, wood frogs, and peepers naturally respond with a need to breed. What's amazing is that all these different creatures get up and go on exactly the same night!

Once they're on the move, different species have different goals. Male salamanders are on a mission: they need to arrive at the breeding pool before the females. Once there, males swim around so their glands can work up a chemical perfume (pheromone) that attracts females. After their eggs are fertilized, females attach them to plant stems and twigs in the water.

Toads and frogs come to the pond to mate and breed, too, but instead of emitting a perfume, male toads and wood frogs call to females with deep, rhythmic sounds. Male peepers call with their characteristic peeps.

What about snakes and turtles? Many types of turtles brumate (that's hibernate in herp talk) under the water. Those that don't, need a good soak almost as soon as they wake up. They'll look for water and food first, then start their mating process.

Snake behavior varies. In some species, snakes spend some time basking in the sun to warm up before traveling. In other species (such as the garter snake), the males leave the den first.

SNAKE ROAD TRAFFIC

 Thirty-five species of snakes and fifteen species of amphibians share the road during migration season on Snake Road. Turtles and lizards also travel. Here are some of the travelers you may see during rush hour.

REPTILES
Western cottonmouth snake
Eastern rough green snake
Diamondback snake
Copperhead snake
Timber rattlesnake
Western mud snake
Black ratsnake
Kingsnake
Black racer snake
Eastern box turtle
Broad-headed skink

AMPHIBIANS
Bullfrog
Chorus frog
Wood frog
Spotted salamander

SNAKE CROSSINGS

Unlike the amphibians, the snakes near Snake Road don't all migrate on the same night. In the spring, some snakes come out to bask in the sun on the rocks for a few hours, then return to their dens at night. This might continue for a few days or weeks before they leave for the swamp for the summer. The females of some species, such as the timber rattlesnake, will even return to their dens in the summer so that they can give birth in a safe place. Their young snakes will remember the den, and will return there in the fall.

When fall migration starts, amphibians close to Snake Road start looking for a place to spend the winter. Toads use their hind legs to dig holes, and salamanders find places in underground tunnels or beneath piles of leaves. But the snakes head to the rocky bluffs, where they'll crawl into cracks in the rocks and stay there until spring.

Snakes may not seem like social creatures, but when it's time to overwinter, many snakes have no problem bunking down with other snakes, even if they're not the same species. These denning places (also called hibernacula) can have from four to a few dozen snakes all coiled up together.

In some places, several hundred snakes will winter together. In other places, several thousand winter together! Since snakes cannot regulate their own body temperatures, hibernating together helps them maintain enough heat to stay alive.

VERNAL POOLS

In the summer and fall, they might look like ditches or hollow places on the forest floor. In the winter, they may be covered with ice. But in the spring, when the winter snow melts and the rains come, temporary ponds called vernal pools appear, filled with just enough water to give frogs, toads, and salamanders

a great place to lay their eggs. The pools aren't deep enough or permanent enough for fish to live in, which improves the odds that the eggs won't be eaten. You can find vernal pools filled with tadpoles during spring hikes in forests or wetlands. By summer, vernal pools have often dried up, and the amphibians that were hatched there have moved on.

ROADSIDE ASSISTANCE

As more and more forested land is developed, many amphibian migration routes cross busy streets. While Snake Road is in a national forest and doesn't see that much vehicle traffic anyway, many roads that amphibians cross have too much traffic to shut them down for long periods of time. Safe passage between hibernation spots and breeding grounds is very important for the long-term survival of many amphibian species. So how can human and herptile traffic share the same roads?

Engineers and biologists came up with a cool solution: if amphibians can't get across a road, why not send them under it? A toad tunnel is just what it sounds like: a tunnel built under a bridge or road that helps toads (and other amphibians) move from their winter hideouts to their breeding grounds. Some tunnels are designed especially to appeal to toads. There are more toads crossing roads than frogs, and toads move more slowly than frogs. Others tunnels have special features that attract salamanders or other types of amphibians. When the tunnels are built correctly, toads and other amphibians use them instead of crossing a road, and more of them live to reproduce. Toad tunnels can be found in many parts of Switzerland, Germany, and the United Kingdom, and they're becoming more popular in the United States with the help of groups such as the National Wildlife Federation.

ROADSIDE ASSISTANCE

Not every area has a toad tunnel. But toads, frogs, and salamanders can still get some migration assistance with the help of amphibian crossing guards. In places across North America, local nature centers and environmental groups organize teams of volunteers to gather at crossing sites to help the migrators safely cross the roads. When the weather calls for rain and warm temperatures, volunteers put on reflective clothing and grab their flashlights, then head out to meeting points to look for herps. Often, volunteers will put up salamander- or frog-crossing signs to warn oncoming cars to slow down. Sometimes, volunteers make bucket brigades or "frog ferries," picking up the salamanders, peepers, wood frogs, and toads and carrying them safely across the road in their hands or in pails or buckets. Check with your local environmental education center to find out if you can train to become an amphibian crossing guard!

A garter snake (above) and a Western rattlesnake (left) on the go

CATCHING UP WITH HERPTILES

Want to see for yourself? Snake Road is closed for vehicle traffic between March 15 and May 15 in the spring and between September 1 and October 30 in the fall. In the spring, the best time to observe amphibians is at night, when temperatures have started to rise above 40°F for a few days and there's rain in the forecast. In the fall, you'll see the most herptiles at the end of a warm day, just as evening temperatures are starting to drop. You can get more information by contacting the Forest Service.

- **Giant City State Park, near Carbondale, Illinois**
  stateparks.com/giant_city.html

- **Snake Dens of Narcisse, near Inwood, Manitoba, in Canada's Prairie Provinces**
  Go online to gov.mb.ca and do a search for "snake dens."

If you can't get to one of these herp havens, look for migrating snakes, frogs, and salamanders in your own neighborhood! The first step is to identify wetlands, ponds, or vernal pools where they're likely to gather. Start looking for these places as soon as the weather gets warm enough. Monitor the weather by checking the temperature daily and finding out when rain is expected. When all the conditions are right, ask your parents if they'll come with you to the spot you've found. Go in the early evening, and be sure to wear reflective clothing and bring flashlights. Look along the edges of the ponds and pools. If there are peepers or other frogs in your area, just follow their throaty calls. If you discover that the herps in your area must cross a busy road to get to their pools, why not put up a temporary sign that warns drivers to watch out for them?

THE PRONGHORN PATH: Life in the Fast Lane

The pronghorn is the original all-American animal. There's no species like it anywhere else in the world. Biologists say that when the first humans arrived on the continent 30,000 years ago, pronghorns had already been here for millions of years.

Back then, the American West looked a lot like the African savanna does today. There were animals similar to modern-day elephants, hyenas, and lions in what's now South Dakota, Wyoming, and Montana.

This area was also home to the American cheetah, the stealthy, speedy animal that was Pronghorn Enemy #1. American cheetahs hid in the tall grasses, waiting to pounce, then chased pronghorns at lightning-fast speeds. American cheetahs disappeared from Earth 10,000 years ago, but pronghorns are, in a way, still running from cheetah ghosts. That's why pronghorns are the second-fastest creatures on the planet, surpassed in speed only by African cheetahs.

With their main predator extinct, pronghorns grew in number. When the first European settlers arrived in the West, as many as forty million pronghorns roamed the plains. One train-traveling pioneer reported seeing a pronghorn herd that stretched for seventy miles—almost as far as the eye could see.

But that soon changed. Settlers hunted pronghorns. Settlers also pulled up the sagebrush pronghorns like to eat to make way for farms. By the 1920s, there were only about 13,000 pronghorns left. With help from wildlife conservationists, that number has increased, and pronghorns are no longer endangered. In Wyoming, they even outnumber people! Dangers still await them, though, on the migration path they take every year, twice a year.

WHERE IS THE PRONGHORN PATH?

Pronghorns can be found as far south as Mexico and as far north as Saskatchewan. North Dakota is the eastern border of their territory. A few herds live as far west as eastern Oregon and

THE MIGRATION PATH

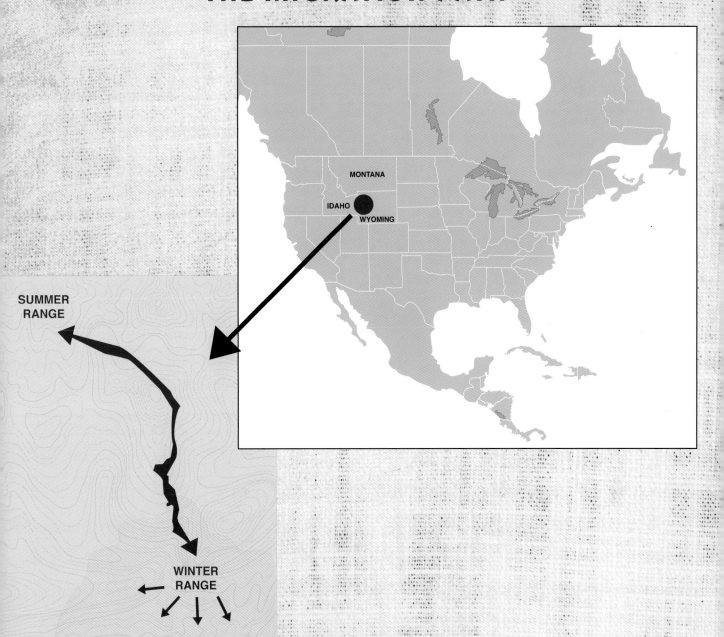

SUMMER
RANGE

WINTER
RANGE

QUICK FACTS

FROM: Summer range in Grand Teton National Park (Lamar Valley)
and Yellowstone National Park

TO: Winter range near Pinedale, Wyoming, and Gardiner, Montana

MILES TRAVELED: 200

SEASONS TRAVELED: Spring and fall

Washington. The pronghorns of Wyoming are the ones that travel the road some people call Antelope Alley.

Every spring since the last Ice Age, pronghorns have followed this road from their winter range in the grasslands and desert to the high mountains of Grand Teton National Park and Yellowstone to get the food they need. Some herds travel more than 200 miles one way, which is the longest migration made by any North American land animal outside of the Arctic Circle. In the fall, they make the same trip back again.

Road Blocks

A lot has changed since pronghorns began migrating. Once, they faced saber-toothed cats, dire wolves, and fierce short-faced bears, all now extinct. Today they might meet coyotes, cougars, and bobcats. However, predators may not be their biggest challenge on the road.

Much of the pronghorn's migration path is now "under construction." The pronghorn's migration path runs near subdivisions, across highways, and over big oil- and gas-exploration sites.

While most humans aren't out to kill pronghorns, human activities and lifestyles have a huge impact on them. Pronghorns are frightened by barking dogs and roaring ATVs (all-terrain vehicles). They have been hit by cars while trying to cross roads.

One of the biggest migration problems for pronghorns is fencing. Millions of years in the grasslands helped pronghorns evolve into fast runners, but it didn't give them any practice jumping. When pronghorns arrive at a fence, they're often too confused to go forward. In some cases, they pile up behind a fence and die of starvation, just a few feet away from a field of food. Pronghorns never jump over fences, but some have learned to go under them if the wire is high enough off the ground. Even if they successfully make it under a fence, pronghorns often lose patches of hair, leaving their skin exposed and vulnerable to winter weather.

Another major problem for migrating pronghorns is what biologists call bottlenecks. Bottlenecks are places where migration paths have become so narrow that they're hard for a herd to pass through. There are places where mountain passages are so narrow that pronghorns travel single-file, following hoof prints from the year before. Down in flatter areas, bottlenecks are caused by roads and development.

Fueling Up

While they're out on the road, pronghorns can go long distances without stopping to eat. When they do eat, these lean, speedy plant-eaters (herbivores) need protein, and they know where to find it.

If a pronghorn and a bison were about to forage in a grassy field, the bison would open its big mouth and just start chowing down on whatever it could find. But a pronghorn would nibble long grasses while searching out forbs (broad-leaf, protein-packed flowering plants) and nutritious shrubs such as sagebrush. Pronghorns have also been known to eat cactus.

While they're finicky eaters, there's one fuel that pronghorns really gobble up: oxygen. Pronghorns run with their mouths open to take in extra air. Their windpipes, hearts, and lungs may be up to four times larger than those of other animals of the

same size, and they have more blood hemoglobin to carry oxygen to their lungs and muscles, too. They also have an unusually high number of power-generating mitochondria in their muscle cells. With these adaptations, pronghorns can burn oxygen at an incredible rate: between six and ten liters a minute. Most animals their size burn less than a quarter of that amount in the same time.

In winter, pronghorns use their front feet to dig their food out of the snow.

TRAVELING IN STYLE

Pronghorns aren't just fast runners—they're graceful. Sometimes their movements look like the long, sleek strides of gazelles. Other times they call to mind the quick hops of rabbits. Biologists discovered that pronghorns can effortlessly shift gears between a jog, a gallop, and a dash. In fact, they observed thirteen different movement styles in pronghorns.

When pronghorns are really racing, their front legs go way back and their rear legs come forward so that both sets of legs are in a horizontal position. For several seconds in each stride, pronghorns are airborne!

In 1804, when Captain Clark of the Lewis and Clark expedition saw herds of pronghorn running for the first time, he wrote that they looked like "a flock of birds taking off in rapid flight."

Biologists believe that the pronghorns' coloring and movement are part of a camouflage strategy to confuse predators. In the time it takes for a predator to figure out where a pronghorn herd is and what it's doing, the pronghorns are already far away.

BUILT FOR SPEED

Like fancy race cars, pronghorn bodies are built for speed. In addition to their enlarged organs and low body fat, they have strong rear muscles, which give their back legs a spring that gets them off the ground.

As they run, pronghorns keep their heads and backs straight, making them more aerodynamic. Pronghorn leg bones are lightweight but strong. Their front hooves are larger than the back ones, and they have built-in shock absorbers— bouncy pads that cushion the leg bones from impact as they run.

Pronghorns don't have collarbones on the fronts of their bodies, which allows for a wider range of front leg movement.

All of these factors give the pronghorn its legendary speed, which earned it the nickname Prairie Speedster.

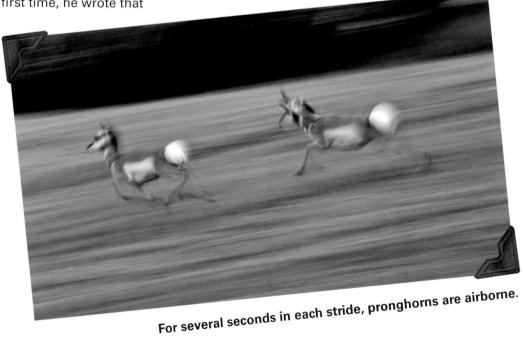

For several seconds in each stride, pronghorns are airborne.

FAST-LANE FACTS

Pronghorns are the fastest mammals in the western hemisphere. They can run up to fifty-five miles an hour for short periods of time. That's the speed limit for cars and trucks on most city roads. When they are just four days old, baby pronghorns can outrun grown-up humans.

Cheetahs—the fastest land animals in the world—are a little faster; they've been clocked at more than sixty miles per hour. But if a pronghorn and cheetah ran a marathon together, the pronghorn would win. Cheetahs are sprinters, but pronghorns are endurance runners.

When they're migrating, pronghorns can travel up to thirty miles a day. Their migration speed is two to three miles per hour.

The cool headgear you see on pronghorns may look like deer antlers, but there are some differences. Antlers grow out of the skulls of deer and are shed every year. Usually only male deer grow antlers. Antelope, goats, and sheep grow horns, which are permanent and aren't shed like antlers. Pronghorns have a kind of hybrid of a horn and an antler. The inside of their headgear is made of bone that never comes off, like a horn. The outside is made of keratin, the same material your fingernails are made from. The outer keratin layer grows, breaks off, and re-grows each year, just like an antler.

Pronghorns have two things in common with skunks: they're both mammals, and they both let off an odor to keep predators away. Just like the skunk, pronghorns have scent glands near their tails. When they sense danger, they let out a strong, goat-like smell.

Pronghorns have binocular-strength eyesight and can spot movement more than three miles away. Although pronghorns are not much larger than goats, their eyes are as large as a horse's. They are set far apart, which makes their field of vision (the area which they can see) very wide. Pronghorns will always see you before you see them.

ROADSIDE ASSISTANCE

Farmers, state agencies, private organizations, the federal government, and non-profits are working together to come up with pronghorn assistance plans.

The fences that stop pronghorns in their tracks usually have barbed wire at the top and bottom to keep sheep and cattle in and predators out. Pronghorn protectors have teamed up with ranchers and sheep farmers to create pronghorn-friendly fences. Barb-free wires that start sixteen to eighteen inches off the ground allow pronghorns to pass safely under. Another type of special fencing lets ranchers control "let-down" wires that can be dropped to the ground as pronghorn herds approach.

Leading pronghorn experts Drs. Kim and Joel Berger have come up with a big idea to help migrating pronghorns: a national migration corridor. The plan would protect the pronghorn's migration path in the same way that other public lands (such as national parks and wildlife refuges) safeguard the animals within their limits. The fence-free corridor would run ninety miles long by one mile wide. Some groups have already pledged to support the plan, but it will take the cooperation of many to make it a reality.

Wildlife biologists have attached radio-tracking collars to pronghorns to trace their movements. These collars have helped researchers create maps of the pronghorns' migration routes, helping them decide exactly which areas need to be protected. If the collars indicate that a group of pronghorns is stopped in one place, the biologists suspect a bottleneck. On one major road that intersects the pronghorns' path, motion detectors have been installed to warn drivers that pronghorns, deer, or other animals are crossing ahead.

CATCHING UP WITH PRONGHORNS

Because they're shy and such fast runners, it can be hard to get a look at pronghorns: They don't really want to be seen. If you do see a pronghorn, don't worry—they're not dangerous and tend to be curious about people. But remember, pronghorns are the second-fastest runners in the world, so one sudden movement and they'll be off.

- **Yellowstone National Park, Wyoming**
  www.nps.gov/yell
  In Yellowstone National Park, pronghorns can be seen near the northern entrance of the park or Lamar Valley in the summer months. In the winter months, you can find them in Gardiner, Montana, just outside the park.

- **Grand Teton National Park, Moose, Wyoming**
  nps.gov/grte/index.htm
  Look for pronghorns in the area known as Timbered Island.

BISON BOULEVARD:
The High Road and the Low Road

Imagine you are a pioneer on your way to settle in Oregon in the 1870s. As your covered wagon rolls through Kansas, you come upon a herd of American bison, also known as buffalo. This herd is so big, you can't see anything else in front of you or to the sides. In fact, it takes six days for you to travel from the beginning of the herd to the end of it!

Biologists say that there were around sixty million bison on the Great Plains during the early 1800s. At that time, bison outnumbered people by more than two to one in North America! When they ran, the Earth shook, so the Native American people called them "the thunder of the plains."

As people moved west in the mid 1800s, the bison's habitat changed very quickly. Railroads cut through the bison's grazing grounds. Settlers pulled up the bison's grass to plant farms. Guns made it easier to hunt bison and kill them in large numbers. By the 1880s, there were almost no bison left. But people, including President Theodore Roosevelt, worked to protect them. Today, about 500,000 bison live in North America.

WHERE THE BISON ROAM
Bison used to live almost everywhere in North America. The only places they didn't live were near the coast or in the desert. Now, most bison live on farms and ranches, although about 20,000 bison live in state and national parks.

Yellowstone National Park is the only wild place left where bison have lived since prehistoric times, and about 4,600 bison live there now. In the summer months, bison graze on the grasses that grow in Yellowstone's high meadows, but in the winter, the meadows may be covered in deep snow. Bison can use their horns to push up to four feet of snow aside to get to the grass they love to eat. When the snow is much deeper than that and they can't get any food, bison begin their annual migration.

THE MIGRATION PATH

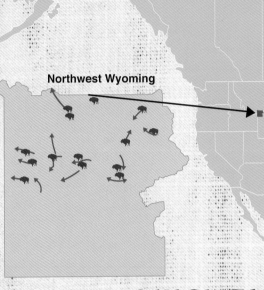

Northwest Wyoming

QUICK FACTS

FROM: Higher elevations in Yellowstone National Park

TO: Lower elevations

MILES TRAVELED: About 40

SEASONS TRAVELED: Late fall and late winter

BISON SHUFFLE

Bison are big. In fact, they are the largest land animal in North America. If you measured from their feet to their shoulders, they can be over six feet tall! They can weigh up to 2,000 pounds, although most are closer to 1,000 pounds. Even though they have a lot of weight to carry, bison can run up to thirty-five miles per hour (about the same speed as a car in a city). Even though they can run fast, they usually don't, traveling only one to two miles a day when they migrate.

   Bison live in herds, but they often split into different types of groups. Females and their calves travel together, and males travel in a separate group. Once they reach their summer grazing grounds, breeding season begins, and males and females come back together. Bison calves are born in the spring and stay with their moms for about a year.

Fueling up

Even though they're huge animals, bison don't "beef up." They're vegetarians, or herbivores, and feed on grasses. They like grass so much that some people call bison the lawnmowers of the prairie! Even though there are a lot of wildflowers on the prairies where they live, bison usually skip them unless there is absolutely nothing else to eat. Pronghorns love to eat these low-growing plants and can often be seen eating side by side with bison, with each getting exactly what they want. Bison eat about twenty-four pounds of food a day!

BISON BITS

The name buffalo came from early explorers who had never seen animals exactly like the bison and confused them with water buffalo found in Asia.

The bison's scientific name is Bison bison.

Bison shed their woolly coats in the summer. That's why you'll often see them with patches of wool hanging off them.

Instead of bathing in water, bison take dirt baths to get rid of the insects that live in their woolly fur. Bison can make big dents in the ground when wallowing in the dust!

Bison may look very serious, but they also have a playful side. Calves run and play together, butting heads, kicking, and racing to build skills they will need as adults.

Bison do not have great eyesight, but they do have a good sense of smell.

Bison have horns and "beards."

The bison we see today are mostly a hybrid, or blend, of the last pure American bison of the nineteenth century and domestic cattle. Only a few herds of genetically pure bison remain in North America. Decades ago, ranchers bred their cattle with pure bison. They hoped that some of the bison's genetic traits, such as size, would make their meat products easier to produce and sell better.

Bison communicate with each other by grunting. If you hear a bison snort or growl, stay away. A grunting bison is in no mood for chitchat and may become aggressive.

Bison were a sacred part of some Native American cultures. The giant animal provided many different peoples with warmth, food, and skin for shelter. In a Lakota legend, white buffalo were symbols of the Great Spirit. Scientifically speaking, white bison have a special condition that causes them to be white and are called albinos.

Road Blocks

Bison face many dangers during and after migration. They share Yellowstone Park with their predators: wolves and bears. Most wolves prefer to eat elk because they are easier to catch, but some wolves specialize in hunting bison. Bison can defend themselves against wolves when they are in a group, so wolves try to separate an old, sick, or young bison from the herd. Bears usually only go after smaller, weaker bison calves.

There is a bigger problem for migrating bison. Some bison carry a bacterial disease that can cause pregnant female cattle to lose their calves. Cattle ranchers in Montana are afraid that bison that leave the park boundaries could infect Montana cattle with the disease. So far, that hasn't happened, but ranchers fear that it will. When bison start to move into Montana in the winter, park officials try to get them back into the park. For many years, they have captured them, brought them back, and kept them in a corral. Some bison are given to local Native American tribes, while others are slaughtered. How can the bison migration be protected and the cattle remain out of risk, too?

ROADSIDE ASSISTANCE

Park officials are searching for new ways to help bison find the food they need without upsetting the ranchers. One idea was a fortified fence that would block the bison from going in certain directions into Montana. But this kind of fence would also affect other animals, such as bighorn sheep, deer, elk, moose, and pronghorns, and could harm the natural habitat.

Another idea was for park officials to leave bales of hay around for bison in the winter so they didn't need to leave the park. Wildlife experts agree, though, that giving animals food from outside their habitat can make them dependent on humans. It's also not good for the environment.

Park officials, conservation groups, and land owners are working together to find a solution that will let the bison roam freely but protect cattle and private land. One idea is to find a place where bison will have enough to eat all year so they don't need to migrate.

A program called Adopt a Wildlife Acre by National Wildlife Federation (NWF) is working well for both bison and ranchers. NWF pays ranchers to give up some of their land grazing rights. The ranchers move their cattle to other places, and the bison get safe grazing space. Other types of wildlife may benefit from this program, too. Where does NWF get the money to pay ranchers? From people who donate money because they care about wildlife.

CATCHING UP WITH BISON

Bison tend to get on the move when the light is low, usually at dusk or dawn, so that's the best time to see them. Bison aren't usually aggressive, but if you see a migrating herd, it's best to keep your distance from them. If they are starting their migration to the lower elevations, they may be weak and not in a very good mood. If they are moving in the other direction, they may be better fed, but you still don't want to get in their way!

- **Yellowstone National Park, Montana;** nps.gov/yell/index.htm
  If you come to Yellowstone in the winter, you might have a chance to see bison on or along the roads north of West Yellowstone, including Highways 191 and 287. During the rest of the year, you will see them in the open grassy fields. Ask your park ranger where you can see the nearest herd!

- **Wood Buffalo National Park, Fort Chipewyan, Alberta, Canada**
  Go online to pc.gc.ca and search for "woodbuffalo."
  This is home to the world's largest herd of free-ranging bison. It starts in the very far northern part of Alberta, and part of the park crosses the border into the Northwest Territories. Visit in the summer when the temperatures are warmer, if you can.

- **National Bison Range, Dixon, Montana**
  fws.gov/refuge/national_bison_range
  About 350 bison live on this range, which was established by President Theodore Roosevelt in 1908. This bison herd is probably the most similar to historical bison.

- **Wind Cave National Park, Hot Springs, South Dakota**
  nps.gov/wica/index.htm
  There are between 250 and 400 bison in the herd at this park. These bison are special because they were never bred with cattle.

POLAR BEAR PARKWAY: Exit North

In the Canadian province of Manitoba, on Hudson Bay, sits a small town called Churchill, which has about 900 residents. As in many small towns in North America, there is only one main street and no traffic light. Unlike in any other small town in North America, you will see some unusual road signs in this town: "Beware of Polar Bear" and "Polar Bear Alert."

Churchill is at the southernmost point of the polar bear's range. Every October, about 1,000 polar bears pass by this town on their annual migration north to the Arctic ice, where they will spend the winter. The town earned its nickname, "The Polar Bear Capital of the World," because it is one of the best places in the world to see polar bears. Every year, as many as 15,000 tourists visit the town to see polar bears gathering on the shoreline, napping, and wrestling each other while they wait for ice to form on Hudson Bay.

GOING WITH THE FLOE

The polar bear's scientific name is *Ursus maritimus,* which means sea bear. The polar bear earned this name because it spends so much time on "pack ice" (also called frozen seawater) on top of the Arctic Ocean. Usually, ice forms on the Arctic Ocean between November and July. During this time, polar bears live on the ice and hunt for seals, their favorite food. They love to eat the seals' blubber, or fat, which keeps them satisfied for a long time.

POLAR BEAR
ALERT

BRRRRR . . .
Polar bears live in five countries: the United States, Canada, Russia, Greenland, and Norway. In the winter, polar bears live in some of the world's coldest places, with temperatures as low as -50°F.

To keep warm, polar bears have layers of fur and a thick layer of fat. Their ears and tails are smaller than those of other animals their size, which lessens heat loss. Polar bears are more likely to overheat than to be cold!

MIGRATION PATH

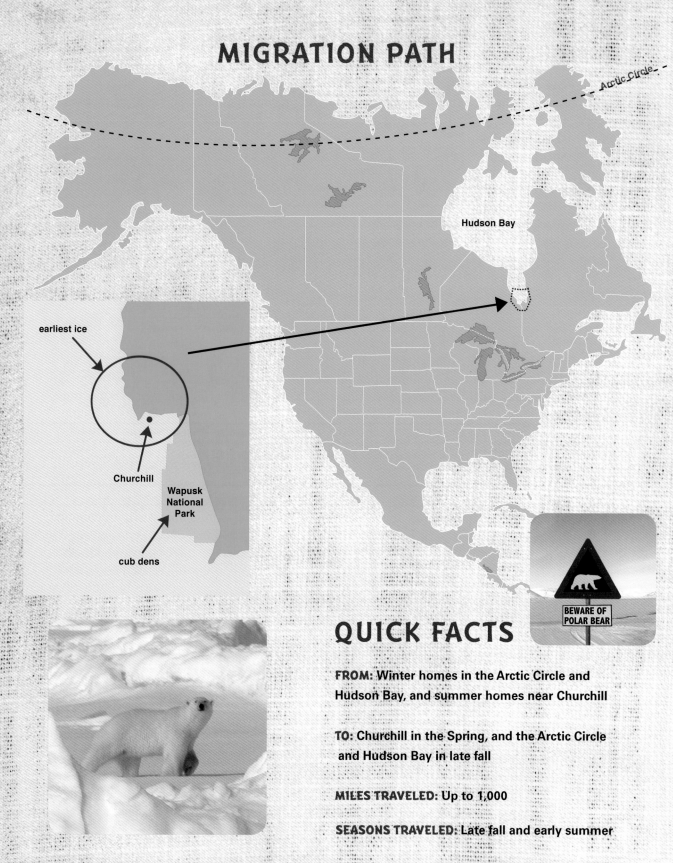

Arctic Circle

Hudson Bay

earliest ice

Churchill

Wapusk
National
Park

cub dens

BEWARE OF
POLAR BEAR

QUICK FACTS

FROM: Winter homes in the Arctic Circle and
Hudson Bay, and summer homes near Churchill

TO: Churchill in the Spring, and the Arctic Circle
and Hudson Bay in late fall

MILES TRAVELED: Up to 1,000

SEASONS TRAVELED: Late fall and early summer

During the early winter, the female polar bear makes a snow tunnel where she will give birth to her cubs. In April or May, the mother polar bear leaves the den to hunt for food for her cubs.

Around June, the ice starts to melt for the season, and polar bears need to find their way to land. On shore, the bears start what biologists call walking hibernation. Although they are awake during this state, there is little food available and their bodies use the fat reserves they stored up during the winter.

Polar bears can wander as far as 1,000 miles during walking hibernation. They eat snow geese and eggs, and caribou if they can find them. They will also eat berries and mushrooms. But none of these foods has enough calories to give polar bears all the energy they need. During the time polar bears are on land, they are really just waiting for the ice to form again so they can get back to the high-energy seal diet that they like the most.

To return to the ice in early winter, the polar bears must swim into Hudson Bay. They are good swimmers, and their fat layer

helps insulate them in icy-cold waters. Biologists say that polar bears can swim for up to 400 miles at a time!

NANOOK OF THE NORTH

Polar bears are very important in the culture of the native Inuit people who live in Arctic Canada. The polar bear has always provided the Inuit people with fur for clothing, meat for food, and skin for rugs. According to tradition, the polar bear gives itself up to the hunter to give him these gifts, and so the people have great respect for the animal and believe it to be sacred. In Inuit legend, the polar bear was called Nanook, and was so powerful that he was almost an equal to humans.

Road Blocks

Each year since 1979, polar ice has begun to freeze later in the fall and winter and melt earlier in the spring and summer. In every decade since that time, 12 percent of polar ice has been permanently lost.

How does this affect polar bears? Biologists who have tracked polar bear migration for many years have made some interesting discoveries. Because of the melting ice, polar bears in the Hudson Bay area now spend thirty days longer on land each year than they did thirty years ago. Each day they spend on land, they lose about two pounds of weight because their land food doesn't provide them with as many calories as seals, their ice food.

Today's polar bears weigh about sixty pounds less than they did thirty years ago. Smaller bears give birth to smaller and fewer cubs, which will affect population sizes in years to come. The number of bears migrating through Churchill has decreased by 22 percent since 1987.

If ice forms later in the year, polar bears face another problem. To get to their icy winter home, polar bears have to swim, which takes a lot of energy. In 2011, biologists tracked one mother bear that had to swim for nine days to get to winter ice. During that time, she lost more than 20 percent of her body weight. Longer swims to and from sea ice can be impossible for cubs because most of them are not strong enough yet to swim such long distances.

Experts say that if climate change continues the way it is now, two-thirds of all polar bears will be gone by 2050. They may even be extinct in the wild by 2100.

INDICATOR SPECIES

Biologists use polar bears as indicator species. This means that when we observe polar bears, we can also learn a lot about other animals and organisms living in the same environment. Polar bears have taught us a lot about the effects of climate change. For example, declining sea ice is already negatively affecting polar bears, which are at the top of the food chain. Other Arctic species might be next. Some, such as ringed seals and walruses, are also showing signs of trouble due to declining sea ice.

Roadside Assistance

The loss of polar bear habitat is a big problem that will not be solved easily. Climate change is caused by greenhouse gases created when we burn fossil fuels such as gasoline. There are many conservation groups working to help save polar bears, including National Wildlife Federation, Polar Bears International, and Defenders of Wildlife.

These groups are working to teach lawmakers about the ways climate change affects the polar region, and asking them to pass new laws. Even though polar bears live in the Arctic, people all over the world are causing the bears' habitat loss. People everywhere must make changes to stop it.

POLAR BEAR PARTICULARS

Polar bears live fifteen to eighteen years in the wild, and into their thirties in captivity. The oldest polar bear known was forty-two and lived in a Canadian zoo.

Newborn polar bears weigh only about one pound and are covered with short, soft fur from the start. Mother polar bears often give birth to twins or triplets. Cubs stay with their mothers for about two and a half years.

Polar bears grip slippery ice with small, raised bumps on their feet called papillae [puh-**pil**-ee].

Polar bear fur isn't really white. It's transparent. Under its fur, a polar bear has black skin that absorbs heat and helps keep the bears warm in frigid Arctic temperatures.

Polar bears' favorite prey are ringed and bearded seals. Ringed seals are small and easy for young polar bears and adult females to catch. The bearded seal is harder to catch, so the larger male polar bears are the ones that are usually successful in hunting them.

Humans are the polar bears' only threat.

Right now, polar bears are called a threatened species. Biologists think there are about 20,000 to 25,000 polar bears left in the world today.

When polar bears are on land, they often wrestle with each other. For cubs, it's a form of play that helps them learn skills they will need to hunt. For adult bears, the wrestling can be real.

Polar bears are the world's largest terrestrial (land) carnivore, with males weighing up to 1,200 pounds and females about half that size. Standing on their hind legs, polar bears can reach eight to ten feet tall, about as high as an official basketball net!

CATCHING UP WITH POLAR BEARS

The best time and place to see polar bears in the wild is in Churchill, Manitoba, between October and November. Tour operators take visitors into the areas outside of town in "tundra buggies" designed especially for polar bear watching. If you can't make it to Churchill, you can watch the polar bear migration on the Polar Bear Cam at explore.org/channels/polar-bears/view-all. Also, check out everythingchurchill.com/experiences/polar-bears/.

PLEASE DON'T PET THE POLAR BEARS!

We think of polar bears as soft and cuddly, but they are wild animals, and humans are their only real threat. Polar bears almost never attack people, but it's still not safe to be near them. To keep polar bears away, residents of Churchill beep their car horns or make other loud noises.

TOO CLOSE FOR COMFORT

Sometimes, bears get too close to Churchill residents and need to be moved to safer places. To relocate bears, wildlife management officers use medicine to relax "too-close-for-comfort" bears. Once they're asleep, the bears are carried in a cargo net attached to a helicopter. The bears are moved a few dozen miles outside of town. Cubs are moved, too, but they get to ride inside the helicopter.

Migration by
SEA

Water looks calm on the surface, but underneath, animals are on the move. Just like land animals, sea creatures move with the seasons.

California gray whales have the world's longest mammal migration. Each year, these gentle giants travel the entire North Pacific coast, from Alaska to Mexico. They are recreating a journey that their ancestors have taken for thousands, or even millions, of years.

Slow-moving manatees do not have a long migration, but it's very important to their survival because they cannot stay in cold waters.

You could say that Pacific salmon were born to run. The annual salmon "run" is their migration from the ocean to the rivers where they were born.

Ready to ride the waves with these spirited sea creatures? Dive into the following pages!

MANATEE TRAIL: No Speed Limit Necessary

In the winter, people from cold climates come to Florida to warm up. Local people call them snowbirds. Just like the birds that fly south for the winter, these folks seem to come in flocks just when northern temperatures drop.

But it's not just birds and people coming to Florida when winter arrives. The West Indian manatee is a marine mammal that makes a short, slow migration each winter, traveling from its home on Florida's Atlantic coast, the Gulf of Mexico, and the Caribbean Sea into warm Florida rivers.

It's not a long trip, and it's not a fast trip. Manatees may even be nature's most laid-back migrators. No rush: we'll get there when we get there! This trip to their winter home is very important to their survival, though. With only about 4,000 West Indian manatees left in the US, their migration isn't just a vacation—it's the journey of a lifetime.

The natural habitat of West Indian manatees starts near the upper Atlantic coast of Florida and extends down into the Caribbean as far south as the northern coast of South America. One manatee was found as far north as Rhode Island! But the warm waters of Florida's coast are home to the largest number of West Indian manatees. Water temperature is a very important factor: when it drops even one or two degrees below 70°F (usually around the beginning of November), manatees are on the move, seeking out warmer water.

Where do they go? From the open ocean, they head toward the Crystal, Homosassa, and Chassahowitzka rivers on Florida's west coast. The water there almost never goes below 72°F. Manatees will cluster around the hundreds of underwater springs in the area. If you know where to find a spring, you'll find manatees nearby.

MANATEES GO GREEN

If you see a manatee up close, you may notice some green or grayish colors on its back and tail. A manatee's tough hide is submerged in water almost all the time, so algae and barnacles grow on it, just as they would on the hull of a boat. These organisms migrate hundreds of miles every year with the manatees!

THE NOSE KNOWS

The manatee's snout is usually the only part of its body that raises above the water. Its nostrils are on the top of the snout. They can be closed tight under water, and opened back up when the manatee comes to the surface for air. Doesn't the manatee's snout look like an elephant's trunk? It acts like one, too. Manatees can grab underwater plants with it to eat!

THE MIGRATION PATH

Tallahassee

Jacksonville

Suwannee

St. Johns

Crystal, Chassahowitzka

Homosassa

Orlando

Gulf of Mexico

Tampa

Lake Okeechobee

West Palm Beach

Fort Myers

Fort Lauderdale

FROM: The Atlantic Ocean, Gulf of Mexico, and Caribbean Sea

TO: The Crystal, Homosassa, and Chassahowitzka rivers

MILES TRAVELED: Up to 200

SEASONS TRAVELED: Early spring and late fall

QUICK FACTS

EASY GLIDERS

Manatees have flat, paddle-shaped tails and two front flippers, each with three or four nails, similar to those you would see on a seal or sea lion. Manatees propel themselves up and down with their tails and use their flippers to steer. They love to roll around sideways, do somersaults, and glide. Even though they're big and bulky, they're true underwater acrobats. Manatees never developed a fast rate of speed because they never had any predators to get away from. They usually travel at around three to five miles per hour. While no one has ever called manatees speedy, they can get around at up to twenty miles per hour if they want to!

Because of their eating habits, manatees are only found in shallow water, but they are equally at home in salt or brackish (part salt, part fresh) waters. They do need fresh water to drink on a regular basis. This is one reason they don't travel farther out to sea: they need to be close to land and fresh water.

To study manatee migration, biologists fitted about 1,400 manatees with radio tags to track their movements. Studies show that manatees move very slowly during their winter migration because they stop to eat so much. They may only move four miles in a whole week! But the tracking devices also showed that one manatee traveled forty-five miles a day for four days.

For the last few decades, manatees have found another type of winter home: near Gulf Coast electrical power plants! While making electricity, these plants release warm water into nearby rivers and the Gulf, making the perfect water temperature for manatees.

Manatees are creatures of habit. Many (but not all) return to the same place each year. Many manatee mothers give birth to their calves in the same place.

Because manatees can live sixty years, several generations of one manatee family can be in the same winter home for about the same time as a human lifetime!

Biologists do not know what cues manatees use to decide when to return to the ocean. They usually migrate back near the beginning of April, when ocean temperatures have increased.

Manatees feeding on algae.

EAT. SLEEP. BREATHE. REPEAT

Manatees are called sea cows because they are herbivores (which means they only eat plants), just like cows. They spend most of their waking time chewing on underwater grasses. They especially like manatee grass (named for them!), which grows in the shallow waters of the Gulf of Mexico, the Caribbean, and the warmer parts of the Western Atlantic. They also eat turtle grass (popular with sea turtles), algae, mangrove leaves, and water hyacinths.

Manatees use their flippers to "walk" along the floor of the river or ocean, find grass, and bring it to their mouths to chew it with their four rows of teeth. Although they're mostly bottom feeders, some manatees feed on leaves from overhanging trees.

Manatees eat up to 150 pounds of grass and other vegetation every day—that's one-tenth of their body weight. No wonder they move so slowly!

Eating so many plants is hard work, so manatees need to rest a lot. They sleep near ocean or river floors, but need to return to the surface every five minutes or so to breathe air. Much of the time, manatees don't even wake up when they go to the surface. They float to the top while still asleep, take in some air, and go back down.

TAKE YOUR TIME

Manatees are slow in more ways than one. Female manatees mature at about five years old, then they have only one calf every two to five years. Male manatees do not mature until they are about nine years old. For manatees, there's really no hurry to grow up!

MORE ABOUT MANATEES

They may have small brains, but manatees are smart! They can easily find warm water, and mother manatees teach their calves to do it, too.

Long ago, sailors mistook manatees for mermaids when they saw their tails swishing under water and nicknamed them la sirena, which means "mermaid" in Spanish. This case of mistaken identity led scientists to name the group of animals to which manatees belong Sirenia. This group also includes their cousin, the Antillean manatee, which also lives in the Caribbean, along the Caribbean coast of Mexico, and Central America. Because the water there is warm year-round, Antillean manatees do not migrate.

Manatee tail

The West African manatee and the Amazonian manatee (which lives in the rivers of northern South America) are also related to the West Indian manatee. The dugong is the manatee's Asian cousin, found in the waters of the South Pacific and Indian oceans. The dugong's tail is fluked (sectioned) like a whale's, and it has a flatter snout than a manatee.

Christopher Columbus saw manatees on his first voyage to the New World.

Manatees are Florida's state marine mammal.

Manatee Appreciation Day is March 26.

Groups of manatees are called cliques.

Manatees have short bristles on their skin.

Manatees are descended from land-walking mammals, and elephants are close relatives!

ROADSIDE ASSISTANCE

CAUTION
MANATEE AREA

Manatees are an endangered species. Some biologists estimate there are only 3,000 to 4,000 left in the United States. Manatees face danger every day, but they face even more risks when they migrate.

Fast-moving boats and slow-moving manatees do not mix. Manatees can be injured by boat propellers. These accidents aren't always fatal, but older manatees often have propeller scars on their bodies. Manatees can also swallow fish hooks, garbage, and fishing line, or get caught in crab traps. There are groups that rescue injured manatees, bringing them back to health then releasing them back into the wild.

Because more than a third of all manatee deaths are caused by boat collisions, the state of Florida has passed strict laws to protect manatees. Biologists say the new laws are working. Boaters are starting to slow down in manatee areas. Plus, manatees are learning to avoid boats.

Habitat loss is the biggest danger to manatees. As more people build houses on the Florida coast, more spring water is used for human needs, making less available for manatees. Some coastal residents do not like vegetation floating on the water in front of their homes, so they clean it from the water, which removes some of the manatees' food.

Several old power plants that once released warm water into rivers and the Gulf have been closed, causing the manatees to lose some of their over-wintering spots.

There are several groups working to protect manatees in Florida. You can adopt a manatee and learn more about them at savethemanatee.org.

CATCHING UP WITH MANATEES

When manatees are out in the Gulf, you can catch sight of them gliding under the water if you're lucky. But you have a better chance of seeing them while they are in their warm-water winter homes.

- **Homosassa Springs Wildlife Park, Homosassa, Florida**
  floridastateparks.org/homosassasprings/
  You can see manatees year-round at this park, where they come to gather around warm springs. This park is also home to manatees that are recovering from injuries or illness.

- **Crystal River, Florida**
  crystalriverfl.org
  There are many different companies in Crystal River that offer manatee tours. With some of them, you can get in the water with the manatees and even touch them, but there are very strict rules to follow.

- **Tampa Electric's Big Bend Manatee Viewing Center, Apollo, Florida**
  tampaelectric.com/company/mvc/
  There is a big electric power plant on Tampa Bay called Big Bend. As part of the process of making electricity, the station releases warm water into the Bay. Manatees discovered this warm water and started to hang out next to the power station all winter long. Built by the electric company, The Manatee Viewing Center has educational exhibits and offers a chance to see the gentle giants up close.

SALMON STREET: Born to Run

Pacific salmon do not have legs, but every year they make a "run" that's one of nature's most incredible voyages. From the open ocean, they travel inland to the river where they hatched from eggs to repeat their life cycle.

To reach their destination, salmon have to avoid fishermen's hooks, bear claws, hydroelectric dams, and harmful chemicals in the water. Swim, flop, and swish along with them for the ride!

Right: Spawning salmon
Far right: Young fish with their egg sacs

THE STARTING LINE

In fall and early winter in British Columbia, leaves fall from the trees and temperatures drop. Many plants and some animals are ending their life cycle. But Pacific salmon are just starting theirs. This is the time of year when salmon spawn, or lay their eggs. The female goes to the bottom of a streambed and turns on her side, fanning her tail back and forth to push gravel aside to form

a nest for her eggs.

After the male fertilizes her eggs, she covers them back up with gravel. She may repeat this process several times, making several nests.

During the winter, the salmon eggs incubate in the nest and hatch a few months later. The newly hatched fish still have their egg sac attached. They stay in the river gravel until spring, when they emerge and are called fry. When they are this small, many fry become prey to predators such as herons, ducks, and other birds. When the fry are big enough, they start the first stage of their journey to the ocean.

FUELING UP

Five species of Pacific salmon plus the related cutthroat and steelhead trout spawn in the North American rivers. (Two more Pacific salmon species spawn in Asia, as well as the Atlantic salmon.) They don't all eat the same food. Once they become adults and swim into the open ocean, some salmon eat microscopic zooplankton, crab larvae, shrimp, squid, and small fish. Chinook eat other fish. Pink salmon eat krill, which gives them the pink color they are named for, and sockeye salmon are filter feeders. From left to right below: squid, crab larva, copepod, and krill.

THE MIGRATION PATH

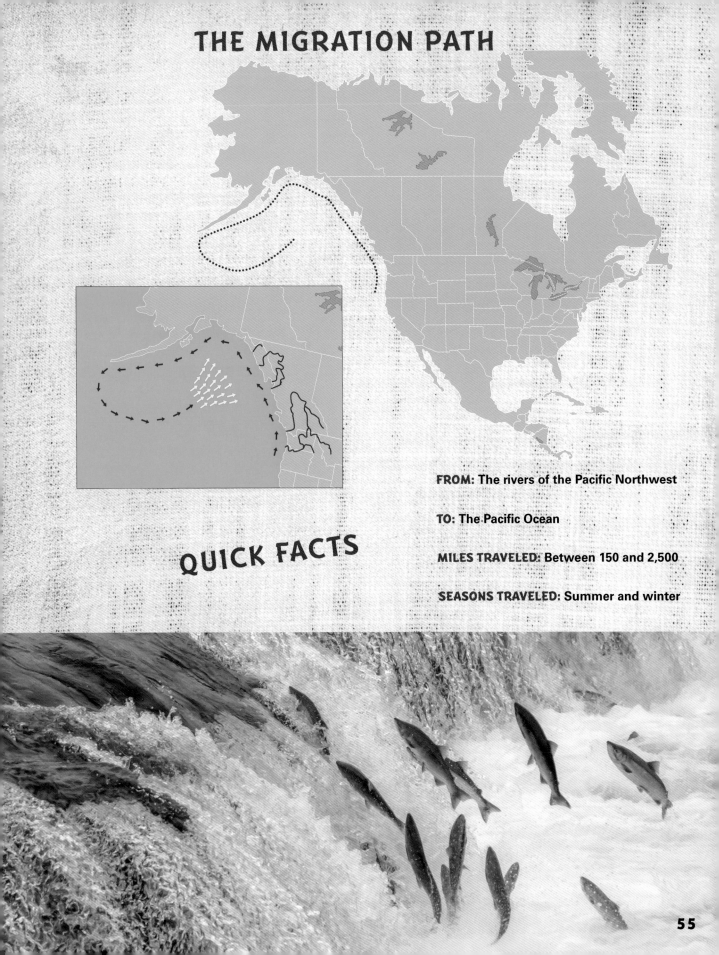

FROM: The rivers of the Pacific Northwest

TO: The Pacific Ocean

MILES TRAVELED: Between 150 and 2,500

SEASONS TRAVELED: Summer and winter

QUICK FACTS

Each type of salmon takes a different path to the ocean. Chum salmon go directly to the sea when they hatch. Pink salmon spend a few months in the estuary and near the shore before moving into the open ocean.

By the time they are ready to enter the ocean, young salmon are at least six inches long, and they're known as smolts. Smolts are covered in a silvery film that protects them from predators and helps them move from freshwater to saltwater. That's just one of the changes their bodies go through to help them transition from being freshwater fish to being saltwater fish. Smolts stick together with other smolts, forming schools. Together, they have a better chance of survival. Once they are in the ocean, they will have many predators, including killer whales and fishermen.

When it's time to enter the ocean, some types of salmon don't go far, preferring to stay near the shore or in the estuaries. These salmon will stay within 150 miles of their hatching sites. But some chinook salmon may travel as far as 2,500 miles and stay out at sea for four to seven years!

THE ROAD BACK HOME

Most salmon spend between one summer and six years at sea. No one knows how they know when it's time, but when they're ready to spawn, salmon start one of Earth's most amazing journeys. From the open ocean, they find their way back to the river where they hatched. Some salmon even return to the exact place of the egg nest they hatched from!

How do salmon know where to go? Once they get close to the river where they were born, they use their noses to pick up a scent that they left behind when they were smolts. Biologists think that they also use celestial navigation, using the sky as a map with the sun guiding them during the day and the stars at night. Biologists also believe salmon use the Earth's magnetic field to identify the mouth of the river where they were spawned. Timing is important. Salmon must be at the mouth of the river at the exact time when the water temperature is right for them.

Just before they get to fresh water, salmon stop eating, and their gills prepare to go back into fresh water. For the rest of their short lives, salmon live on stored body fat and protein.

Road Blocks

The salmon run is a dangerous journey. Salmon may travel forty-five miles per day to get back to their spawning grounds, taking anywhere from a week to months to get there. Along the way, salmon have to overcome what biologists call the "four Hs": habitat destruction, hydroelectric dams, harvesting, and competition with hatchery fish.

As more people live in the salmon's habitat area, there is more runoff into freshwater streams. That means that as rainwater runs from farms, roads, and bridges into the streams, it brings with it sediment that may include toxic chemicals or other substances that can harm salmon. Erosion is also a problem for salmon. When people remove trees from the landscape, dirt washes into streams and settles in the streambeds, disrupting egg nests.

Climate change has also had an effect on salmon. They need their freshwater homes to be below 70°F to thrive. With climate change, the water temperatore in some places has risen dangerously high for them.

On the way back to the nests they hatched in, salmon often need to travel past hydro-electric plants by hurling themselves into the air and climbing "fish ladders" built to help them. These hurling actions take so much energy that salmon weaken or even die from the process. Salmon also have to "climb" waterfalls, jumping from pool to pool through rapids and swimming against strong currents. Eagles and bears watch as they do, waiting to pounce. If the animals don't get them, fishermen often do. Because people are so familiar with the salmon's migration, people who like to fish know where to find them at specific times of the year. As salmon swim upstream, they are easy prey for nets and hooks.

Only a small percentage of salmon that start their migration journey make it back to their spawning ground. They are thin because they haven't eaten since entering fresh water. Their fins are often torn, and many have fishing hooks in their mouths. But they are not safe yet. Once back at the spawning area, it's every salmon for itself. Female salmon fight each other for nesting places, and males fight each other to mate with females.

After all this effort, it's not surprising that most salmon die just days after laying and fertilizing their eggs. When the salmon die, they float downstream, and the nutrients in their decomposing bodies help feed other plants and animals. Steelhead trout live to make the journey again. Those that live are called kelts, and they return once again to the ocean to repeat the process for up to nine years.

Above: Salmon need help to get by the Bonneville Dam on the Columbia River on the Oregon-Washington border.

Below: A "fish ladder" helps salmon on the way back to their birthplace.

In one final twist, many salmon must compete for nesting places with hatchery fish, those that were spawned in human-made fish hatcheries. Each river has enough nutrients to support only a certain number of fish, so for the spawn to be successful, there must be enough nutrients to go around. With hatchery fish coming in, a smaller percentage of eggs in each nest will receive enough nutrients.

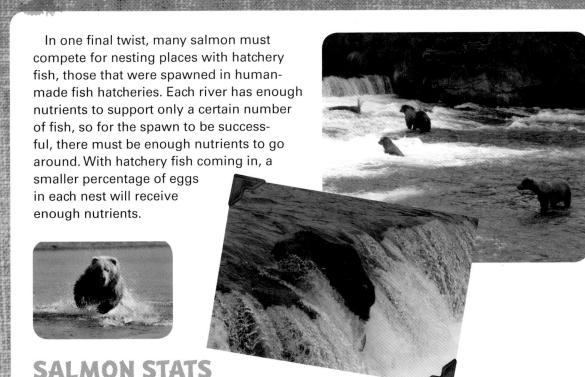

SALMON STATS

The five types of Pacific salmon include: chinook, chum, coho, pink, sockeye, plus cutthroat, and steelhead trout. Pacific salmon are cousins of Atlantic salmon, a group that includes sturgeon, lampreys, and shad.

Sockeye, coho, and most chinook spend between one and two years in freshwater before heading out to sea.

Chinook salmon are also known as king salmon because of their size. They average twenty-four pounds, but some have been known to grow up to one hundred pounds!

Salmon can leap up over six feet in the air! Deep pools help the salmon get a running start so they can leap higher up steep waterfalls.

Less than 3 percent of fish are known to migrate, so salmon are very special!

A salmon's skin changes color during different stages of its life as it moves from freshwater to saltwater. Male and female salmon of the same species are often different colors and don't look very much alike.

Pink salmon are called humpbacks because they develop a large hump on their backs before they spawn.

ROADSIDE ASSISTANCE

For thousands of years, Native American groups in the United States and First Nations groups in Canada have depended on salmon for food. In the nineteenth century, many salmon species were over-harvested. In recent years, damage to their habitat has also threatened Pacific salmon.

Several groups are working to protect Pacific salmon, and they are helping spread the word about the ways that people can pitch in. Efforts to help the salmon have increased their numbers in the past few decades. Here are some ways people can help salmon:

- Buy wild salmon to eat instead of farmed salmon. Farm salmon compete with wild salmon for habitat and food. They can also disrupt the wild salmon's spawning grounds.

- Be careful about how much electricity you use. An increased demand for electricity increases demand for more hydroelectric power.

- Don't use pesticides in your garden. Run-off from gardens and farms ends up in local watersheds or rivers. Those toxic chemicals hurt and kill fish.

Fish biologists use mark-and-recapture studies to learn about salmon migration. They carefully remove fish from the water and tag them. Above: An on-site marking station for young salmon on the Columbia River in Oregon. Top: Biologists catch salmon for tagging in Big Creek, Idaho.

CATCHING UP WITH SALMON

Seeing salmon flop out of the water and into the air on their migration journey is an amazing experience. You can catch up with Pacific salmon in the following places.

- **Ballard Locks, Seattle, Washington**
  seattle.gov/tour/locks.htm
  The viewing area at these locks has a glass window to the fish ladder, allowing visitors to watch salmon on their way back up the river.

- **Bonneville Dam, Cascade Locks, Oregon**
  nwp.usace.army.mil/Locations/ColumbiaRiver/Bonneville.aspx
  Chinook and coho salmon pass up the ladders here. They can be viewed through large windows inside the dam's visitor center, which is located about forty miles from Portland, Oregon.

- **Adams River, British Columbia, Canada**
  salmonsociety.com
  During October, it's possible to see millions of sockeye migrating along this river!

- **Fraser River, British Columbia, Canada**
  gofishbc.com/about-us/what-we-do/fish-hatcheries.aspx
  Sockeye enter this river by the tens of thousands each fall.

THE GRAY WHALE WAY: Baja or Bust

Standing at Point Reyes Lighthouse in California, you scan the horizon and see nothing but water in every direction. Then, something catches your eye: a quick flash! A whale fluke breaches the surface. Just a few seconds later, a spray of water shoots into the air, followed by two more quick sprays. You've just seen one of the ocean's most interesting animals on the trip of a lifetime. You've seen a migrating gray whale.

Each year, California gray whales make one of the world's longest animal migrations. Their trip from Alaska to Mexico and back is about 10,000 miles long and helps them do the two most important tasks in their lives: feeding and breeding.

FEEDING

Starting around May, gray whales can be found in the cold, shallow waters of the North Pacific Ocean and the Bering Sea, between Alaska and Russia. Here, they do what they do best: put on weight. They dive to the ocean floor, flip onto their sides, and suck sediment into their mouths. They filter their food through a baleen, a body part that looks like a big scrub brush and acts like a sieve. Small shrimp-like crustaceans called amphipods are trapped by the baleen, then swallowed by the whales.

For the next five months, the ocean floor turns into a kind of all-you-can-eat buffet where the California gray whales feast. By the time they are done, each

whale has eaten about sixty-seven tons of crustaceans. That's about the weight of a passenger ferry! The gray whale uses the food to build up a layer of blubber about five to six inches thick. The blubber keeps the whales warm in cold water, and also stores energy for the many months of the year when they will not eat much.

THE MIGRATION PATH

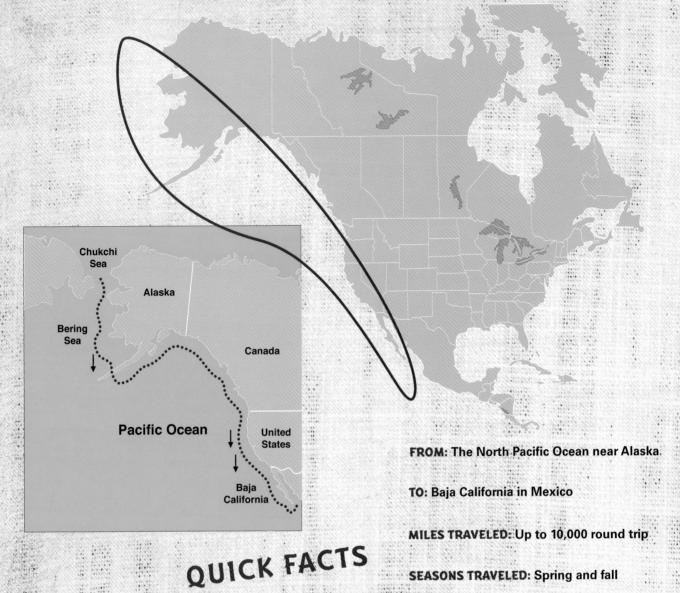

Chukchi
Sea

Alaska

Bering
Sea

Canada

Pacific Ocean

United
States

Baja
California

FROM: The North Pacific Ocean near Alaska.

TO: Baja California in Mexico

MILES TRAVELED: Up to 10,000 round trip

SEASONS TRAVELED: Spring and fall

QUICK FACTS

PROCEEDING

Around October, the feast is over. The water temperature in the North Pacific really starts to drop. The gray whales are about to start a trip that will take them two to three months to complete. During this trip, they will lose about 30 percent of their body weight. Their journey has an important purpose: female gray whales only give birth in one place, in the calving lagoons, or whale nurseries, off the coast of Baja California, Mexico.

Leaving on their journey, the whales travel south in small groups called pods. Swimming at the not-so-fast speed of about six miles per hour, they make about eighty to one hundred miles of progress each day. They usually stay within two and a half miles of the coast along the way. They eat very little as they go, swimming day and night. Sometimes they mate along the way.

The whales swim the entire length of the West Coast of the United States, finally reaching their destination in Mexico in January. There, they swim into shallow waters that offer protection from sharks.

BREEDING

Almost all gray whales spend the winter in one of three lagoons in Baja California. Scammon's Lagoon is named for the whale hunter who discovered the lagoons and who later became the whales' protector. The other lagoons are called San Ignacio and Magdalena.

Female gray whales are pregnant for a year, and then they give birth to a single baby, called a calf. Calves are about thirteen feet long and weigh about 2,000 pounds (the weight of a small car) when they are born. Some calves are born before their mothers reach Mexico. When that happens, you may be able to see newborn whales migrating, too!

A calf drinks fifty gallons of its mother's milk every day. Mother whales take care of their young for about eight months. When they are little, you may even see a baby riding on its mother's back!

In February and March, the males and single female whales start to leave the lagoons, returning north to their feeding

grounds near Alaska. The pregnant and nursing mother whales stay in the lagoons until they sense that their calves are strong enough to make the journey, which is usually around mid to late March. Then the cycle of life starts all over again for the California gray whales.

THE WAY OF THE GRAY

Gray whales have some unusual behaviors that biologists do not completely understand yet. They breach or jump up out of the water, making a big splash when they come down. Biologists think it might be a form of play or a way whales communicate with each other.

Gray whales also stick their heads out of the water, an activity researchers call spyhopping. There are a few theories about why they spyhop. If they hear better out of water, they may be listening for surf sounds to ensure they are still near the coast. When you have a chance to see a gray whale, it is usually because

the whale is lobtailing, which is when a whale lifts its tail out of the water and slaps it on the surface. Lobtailing makes such a loud noise that biologists believe gray whales use it for communication.

WHAT DO YOU KNOW ABOUT GRAY WHALES?

Gray whales live for almost as long as humans. The average gray whale lives between fifty-five and seventy years!

Gray whales are called baleen whales because of the bristle-like brush in the front of their mouths that helps filter their food. Baleen whales also have two blowholes. When they surface, they breathe for three or four breaths in a row, then go back under water for three to seven minutes.

Adult gray whales can grow to about forty-nine feet long. That's about four feet longer than the size of an average school bus. They can weigh up to thirty-six tons, or about the weight of an armored vehicle. Even though that seems big, they are medium size for baleen whales.

Gray whales have bumps, or "knuckles," on their backs instead of a dorsal fin.

As mammals, gray whales are more closely related to other mammals such as cows than they are to fish. The gray whale can be traced directly back to a whale that evolved more than thirty million years ago. It's the only living species in the genus Eschrichtius.

During the days of whaling, gray whales were called devilfish because they violently thrashed when they were harpooned by hunters. Now, they are called las amistosas *by many local Mexicans, which translates to "the friendly ones," because they sometimes approach boats and let people touch them when they are in the nursery lagoons.*

Gray whales can stay under water for about fifteen minutes before they need to surface for air.

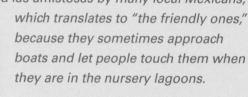

Left: This young gray whale was photo-graphed up close when it surfaced near a whale-watching tour boat.

Road Blocks

In the nineteenth century, whalers discovered that gray whales spent their winters in the shallow waters near Baja California. Here, they were easy targets, and they were hunted almost to extinction. But new laws were passed to protect the whales, and now the population on the eastern North Pacific is healthy. But on the other side of the Pacific, near China and Korea, researchers know of fewer than 100 gray whales.

Researchers found that in 1979, about forty whales per hour passed Point Reyes in California during peak migration time. Now, only about eight whales an hour pass the same area during the peak. Biologists believe that there are fewer whales because the increase in whale-watching boats and other boat traffic has caused the whales to shift their migration farther out to sea. Boaters are not allowed within one hundred yards of whales, but sometimes there are dozens of whale-watching boats near a pod at the same time.

The gray whale's main predator is the orca. Orcas often prey on gray whale calves as they are migrating, so mother whales keep their babies close. In the calving lagoons of Mexico, great white sharks might also occasionally prey upon calves. Humans are their only other predator. Some native peoples in Alaska have the legal right to hunt gray whales because of cultural traditions.

Whale Weather Alert

Like the polar bear, the gray whale's migration is affected by global climate change. The amphipods that gray whales eat are carried on sea ice and dropped by ocean currents in the places where gray whales find them. If the ice doesn't form in that area, the amphipods won't be there, either. One year, a large number of gray whales died of starvation because they couldn't find amphipods.

For a few years, biologists have noticed that gray whales have been staying in the cold northern waters longer, and they seem to be gaining less weight. This can affect the whales in two ways. If females don't get enough to eat, they may not be able to have babies. If the adults are too thin when they start their migration south, they may be vulnerable to orca attacks.

Several other problems affect gray whales. Sonar from military, commercial, and recreational boats may disturb them. Oil and gas exploration along the migration corridors can disrupt their routes, and bottom-trawling boats destroy their food source.

When a gray whale dies during its migration, the carcass can provide food for many land animals if it washes ashore. Polar bears can smell a whale carcass up to twenty miles away.

ROADSIDE ASSISTANCE

Many laws have been passed to help gray whales on their migration route. Boats are not allowed to get too close to the whales, and those that break this rule must pay a fine. Wildlife organizations are also working to get laws passed to prevent boats from trawling or using sonar in the whale's feeding areas.

CATCHING UP WITH GRAY WHALES

There are many places along the California coast where you can see gray whales during their journey. The trick is to be at the right place at the right time and to know what to look for. During January, the whales head south, so if you see a fluke (whale tail) exit the water briefly, the next place it will surface will be to the south.

You can tell if a whale has recently surfaced because you can see a "footprint" in the water, which looks like a circle of still water surrounded by water that is rougher. You can see whales in a lot of locations all up and down the coast, but these are a few of the most popular places to catch up with migrating gray whales.

- **Whale Watching Center, Depoe Bay, Oregon**
  Go to <u>oregonstateparks.org</u> and search for whale watching.
  You can watch for whales almost year-round at this state park. The peak time for cold-weather migration is mid-December to January. In spring, you're most likely to see whales returning to the north from March through June, and in the summer and fall between July and November.

- **Point Reyes National Seashore, Point Reyes Station, California**
  <u>nps.gov/pore/planyourvisit/wildlife_viewing_whales.htm</u>
  The best time to see southbound whales here is in January. Late March and April are peak times for seeing northbound whales.

- **Point Piedras Blancas, San Simeon, California**
  <u>piedrasblancas.org/research.html</u>
  From July through November, you can see the whales close to shore here. You can also see them on their way south from Alaska starting in November.

- **Cabrillo National Monument, San Diego, California**
  <u>nps.gov/cabr/historyculture/old-point-loma-lighthouse.htm</u>
  You can see gray whales passing here between December and March about three-fourths of a mile out to the horizon. Remember, they are migrating south, which is to your left as you look west out over the ocean from Cabrillo National Monument. Once you spot a whale, you can expect that it will surface again to the south moments later.

Migration by SKY

Look up! At certain times of the year, you may see birds in large flocks above your head, flying from their homes in the north to the south for the winter. Many other winged animals take to the sky in different seasons for different reasons.

The sandhill crane is a large bird that travels from Texas and points farther south to Canada, Alaska, or even Russia, stopping on the Platte River in Nebraska along the way. What makes this migration so special is the number of birds: There may be 500,000 in just one month!

Monarch butterflies make the world's longest insect migration. From their forest homes in Mexico and southern California, monarchs fly north each spring in search of milkweed. By fall, their great-great-grandchildren will fly back to the very same trees to spend their winter, guided by invisible markers that biologists don't quite understand yet.

Ready to fly with some of the Earth's most amazing winged creatures?

THE CRANE CORRIDOR:
Rush Hour in the Sky

Flocks of the long-necked, long-legged sandhill crane take to the sky each spring. That's not so different from what many birds do, but the sandhill crane's migration is very special. It's one of the world's only animal migrations in which between 80 to 90 percent of an entire species on the planet is in one place at the same time! Between March and April each year, around 500,000 sandhill cranes travel up what's called the Central Flyway—from Texas, New Mexico, and Mexico—on their way to their breeding grounds in Canada, Alaska, and as far away as eastern Siberia.

Some types (subspecies) of sandhills stop for one month along the Platte River in Nebraska. In a seventy-five-mile area, the birds gather to feed and rest. In some places, there are as many as 12,000 birds resting in an area just one-half mile long! How and why do they get there? It's a fascinating story.

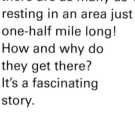

A CRANE'S WAY

In the winter, migrating sandhill cranes live in shallow lakes and rivers in Mexico, Arizona, New Mexico, and Texas. They live in big flocks here until around early February, when they begin their long journey north to their breeding grounds where they will spend the summer. How do they know it's time to go? Biologists still aren't sure, but they think it has to do with the amount of daylight and the cranes' nutritional needs. The first cranes begin to fly away in groups as small as fifteen and as large as one hundred, all heading north and following the same invisible air paths. Soon, thousands of cranes join them.

Cranes migrate during the daytime, riding on rising columns of warm air called thermals which help push them forward. They ride these winds up to a few thousand feet high, gliding along until they find the next thermal and spiral upward again. Moving this way helps them save energy because they don't have to flap their wings as often when they glide. Unlike geese, cranes often migrate at such a high altitude that people can't see them from the ground.

THE MIGRATION PATH

lesser
sandhill
crane

Canadian
sandhill
crane

QUICK FACTS

FROM: Mexico and the American Southwest

TO: Canada, Alaska, and Siberia

MILES TRAVELED: As many as 5,000

SEASONS TRAVELED: Spring and fall

Migrating cranes usually fly about 200 to 300 miles a day, and tracking data has shown that some cranes can fly as far as 500 miles a day! Cranes have a good sense of the weather. If they sense a storm coming, they roost in trees until it passes.

As night falls, cranes look for resting sites in wetlands. When the sun rises, they leave again, repeating this process daily. The cranes start to arrive in late February. By late March, there are tens of thousands of cranes along the Platte River.

During their time on the river, the cranes wake up each morning by calling to each other with their well-known trumpet call. The business of each day is to eat leftovers from local farm fields. Their daily foraging flights help keep their muscles in shape for the long journey that's still ahead of them. Around sunset, the cranes gather together again around the river to sleep.

Most migrating cranes spend about twenty-nine days in the Platte River Valley. Almost all at once and almost exactly on April 10, the cranes take off again. Only a few stay around until May. By that time, they are all on their way north again. Interestingly, the cranes will pass through the Platte River area again in the fall, on their way south for the winter, but not in the same numbers. That one month in spring is the only time of year they can be found together.

SONG & DANCE SANDHILL CRANE STYLE

While they are on their Platte River stopover, sandhill cranes have some important business to do. They are there to mate, and they mate for life. The sandhill crane mating dance (below) is unique. They bow, stretch out their wings, and leap into the air. Sometimes they even pick up sticks or corncobs and throw them up and down with their bills to impress their mates. Courting cranes follow each other's lead in how they dance. The male lets out a few loud honks. The female follows. The two jump up and down and call loudly to each other. It's really something to see!

Fueling Up

Sandhill cranes are omnivores, meaning they eat both plants and animals.

They are also opportunistic feeders, which means they will eat whatever they can get. They like to eat grains that grow on farms, and about 90 percent of their diet during migration is what's called waste corn (the corn that falls to the ground during the fall corn harvest). All together, cranes eat about 1,600 tons of corn while they are in the Platte River Valley. But they also eat wheat and sorghum. They use their bills to pull plants out of marshy waters and eat them. They also eat frogs, earthworms, snails, and insect larvae.

While they are in the Platte River Valley, most cranes put on a pound of fat, which provides the energy and water necessary to complete their migration and begin nesting.

Road Blocks

When you read that there are half a million sandhill cranes in one place at one time, you may not think that this species is in any danger of disappearing. There are many threats to the cranes, though.

Habitat destruction is the biggest problem for cranes. They need wetlands for breeding and roosting sites, but many wetland habitats are being filled in with land for human developments. Dams along rivers have provided water for farmers' fields, but this makes rivers narrower, so there's less

water for the birds.

Habitat fragmentation is another type of habitat destruction the cranes face. In the cranes case, their habitat has been broken up by human development, such as roads and dams. These smaller habitat areas cannot support large crane populations.

Another problem for the sandhill crane is that snow geese stop along the Platte River on their migration route, and their population sizes are increasing. The geese also feed on waste corn in the fields, creating competition for this important food.

Invasive species can also be harmful to the cranes' food sources along the river. When a new non-native plant starts to spread in the cranes habitat, the native plants that the cranes eat are less plentiful.

SANDHILL STATISTICS

Cranes are some of the oldest living birds on the planet! Some crane fossils found in Nebraska date back nine million years, long before the Platte River was formed.

There are six subspecies (types) of sandhill cranes, but only three of them migrate.

Sandhill cranes can be three to four feet tall with six- to seven-foot-wide wingspans!

Sandhill cranes can live more than twenty-five years.

Male cranes are called roans. Female cranes are called mares.

One unique thing about sandhill cranes is the noise they make. Their tracheas are shaped like saxophones which amplify the sound they make. When many cranes honk at the same time, the sound can be heard over a mile away.

Sandhill cranes have been seen flying over Mt. Everest!

Since the middle of the twentieth century, the number of sandhill cranes migrating over Nebraska has increased. Biologists think this increase is because of corn crops. Cranes can find more corn here, so more of them choose this migration route.

COOL DISGUISE

Some sandhill cranes dip their bills in water, searching for plants covered with iron oxide. They rub the leaves on their feathers, which gives them a reddish color. Sandhill cranes are one of the few species known to color their feathers on purpose. Biologists believe they do this to camouflage themselves from predators such as bobcats, wolves, hawks, and eagles.

ROADSIDE ASSISTANCE

Many groups are working to protect the sandhill crane's habitat and its migration routes. Biologists have tagged the legs of migrating cranes so that the birds can be tracked on their migration. Some wear brightly colored plastic bands so they can be seen from a distance with binoculars, but others are tagged with radio transmitters. By tracking their movements, biologists hope that they will be able to understand the threats cranes face and find ways to protect them.

FOLLOW THE LEADER
Ultralight planes can be used to teach young whooping cranes their migration path when their parents cannot. The endangered whooping crane is a close cousin to the sandhill crane.

CATCHING UP WITH CRANES

People who have seen cranes along the Platte River during their migration say that you cannot believe how amazing it is unless you see it. In addition to cranes, more than two million snow geese migrate along the cranes flyway, as well as ducks, bald eagles, hooded mergansers, and the endangered whooping crane (there are only a few hundred of them left in the world). The sights, sounds, and smells of these birds are unforgettable! Here are some of the best places and times to get the experience.

- **Rowe Sanctuary, Gibbon, Nebraska**
  rowe.audubon.org
  If you arrive here at sunrise or sunset during March and April, you're bound to catch sight of a good number of sandhill cranes. If you're extremely lucky, you may even see some whooping cranes, too.

- **Jasper-Pulaski Fish and Wildlife Area, Medaryville, Indiana**
  in.gov/dnr/fishwild/3091.htm
  The cranes pass through this area on their fall route south. The best time to catch them here is late October through mid-December, at sunrise and sunset.

- **Crane Meadows National Wildlife Refuge, Little Falls, Minnesota**
  fws.gov/refuge/crane_meadows
  Cranes flock here in late March and early April, gathering in the wetlands to nest. Cranes that nest farther north may stop over here on their way back south in fall.

THE MONARCH FLYWAY: The Great Glide

Looking at a spring garden, you may see butterflies swirling around, coming to rest on your flowers, and then fluttering away. If you see one with orange-and-black patterned wings, you may be looking at a monarch on the trip of a lifetime. Monarch butterflies make what is believed to be the world's longest insect migration, traveling from parts of North America as far north as Canada to as far south as central California and Mexico.

Monarchs weigh less than half a gram, about the weight of a paperclip. They may be tiny, but they are mighty. On their journey, some monarchs travel up to 2,500 total miles and up to fifty miles a day. For some monarchs, the journey can take two months.

Monarchs are found flying solo during the daytime, but at night they often "cluster" with other monarchs. So, while you may only see a few monarchs at a time in your garden, these few are part of a much bigger movement going on all around you.

TAKE TO THE SKY

North American monarchs migrate to complete different phases of their life cycle. During the spring and summer, you can find monarchs anywhere you find milkweed plants across the United States and in some parts of Canada.

While in their northern homes, monarchs search for milkweed plants. Females lay their eggs on the undersides of milkweed leaves and die shortly after.

When the eggs hatch, the caterpillar larvae feed on milkweed leaves. The leaves contain a chemical that builds up in the caterpillars bodies, making them taste terrible to predators. The caterpillars feed on milkweed until they enter their chrysalis stage to develop into butterflies.

MONARCH LIFE STAGES
Left to right: Caterpillars emerging from eggs, caterpillar, chrysalis, and an adult emerging from its chrysalis

THE MIGRATION PATH

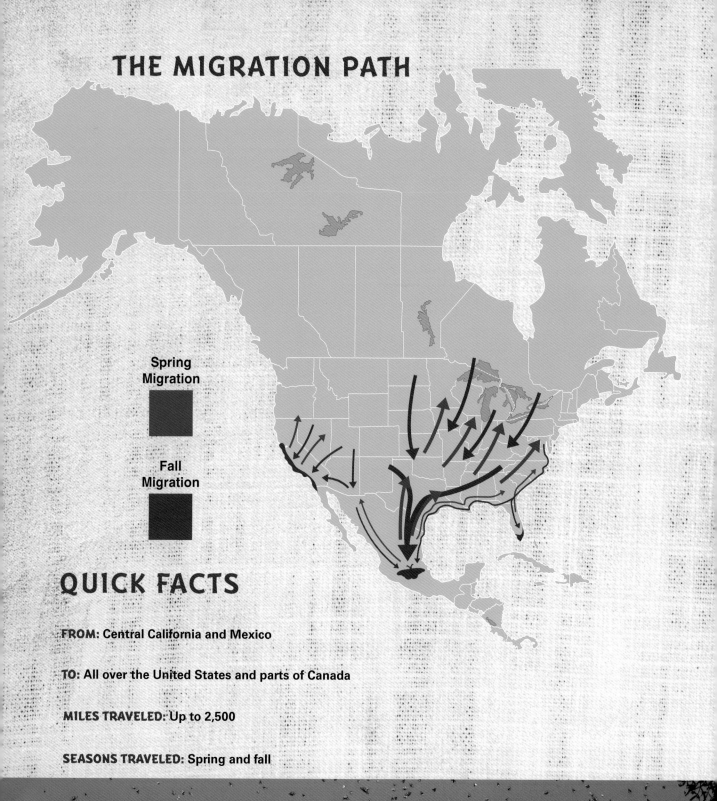

Spring
Migration

Fall
Migration

QUICK FACTS

FROM: Central California and Mexico

TO: All over the United States and parts of Canada

MILES TRAVELED: Up to 2,500

SEASONS TRAVELED: Spring and fall

Four generations of monarchs can grow and die within one summer. The first three generations live from two to six weeks. Each generation moves a little farther north, continuing to mate and lay eggs. The fourth generation can live up to nine months. This is the generation that will migrate south.

When the seasons start to turn (usually around September or October), the fourth-generation monarchs leave their homes and start the long migration to warmer places, where they will spend the winter.

Monarchs that live east of the Rockies travel to a single forest of oyamel fir trees in Mexico's Sierra Madre. Tens of millions of butterflies arrive in this forest each fall! The trees full of butterflies seem to quiver with life—the layers of monarchs make the trees look as if they're made from swirls of orange and black.

Monarchs that live west of the Rockies travel to central California, clustering on top of each other in eucalyptus trees along the Pacific Coast in large mounds that seem to sway in the wind.

Biologists are not sure why (or how!), but monarchs return not just to the same area, but also to the very same trees each year. It's curious because the monarchs that return to the south are not the same ones that journeyed north the year before. Experts believe the monarchs may be leaving a chemical scent on the trees that new generations will use to recognize the right place.

In their overwintering place, monarchs go into a semi-dormant state. In the spring, when temperatures become warmer and days become longer, the monarchs leave to find a place to lay their eggs. How do they know it's time to leave? Biologists believe the monarchs use natural cues such as

temperature and amount of daylight.

How many monarchs make the great glide? Biologists have tracked monarch migrations for about twenty years. On average, abut 360 million monarchs make annual migrations, but each year the number decreases.

Fueling Up

When they are in the larval (caterpillar) stage, the monarchs' diet is made up entirely of milkweed, a wildflower that doesn't grow in Mexico. When they're

adults, monarchs drink the nectar from flowers, which they store as fat in their abdomens.

As they begin their journey, monarchs depend on this stored fat to fuel them for up to 2,500 miles! Along the way, they drink nectar wherever they can find it. Even though they are traveling up to fifty miles a day, monarchs gain weight on their trip. They conserve energy by gliding along the way, catching air currents to propel them forward.

MONARCH MISCELLANY

The colors on monarch wings aren't for decoration: They send a message to predators to stay away. The monarch is poisonous to eat because as a caterpillar its diet consists solely of milkweed, a plant that contains toxins. Monarchs are immune to these toxins, but other animals that might want to eat them are not. These toxins become stored in the monarch's body.

Mexico's Purepecha people call monarchs the "souls of the departed" because monarchs return to Mexico near the Day of the Dead, a holiday that honors ancestors.

Monarchs can also be found in the Pacific Islands, Australia, and parts of western Europe.

Monarchs aren't the only butterflies that migrate long distances, but they are the only ones that migrate as part of their life cycle. The monarchs that make the trip south in the winter are the great-grandchildren of the ones that came north.

Monarch butterflies cannot fly if their body temperature is lower than 55°F. They will sit in the sun or "shiver" their wings to warm up.

The monarch is the state insect or butterfly of Alabama, Idaho, Illinois, Minnesota, Texas, Vermont, and West Virginia.

Road Blocks

Even though there are still millions of monarchs making their yearly journey, there are many fewer than there were in the past. There are several reasons the monarch population is decreasing so quickly.

MILKWEED

Monarchs need milkweed to survive, but many U.S. farmers view milkweed (below) as a weed that competes for crop space. They use herbicides to kill it. In the past ten years, more than twenty-four million acres of milkweed have been lost in the United States, which means monarchs have a much harder time finding food and places to lay eggs.

LOGGING

Logging in Mexican forests has reduced overwintering sites for monarch. Without shelter the butterflies are also more vulnerable to weather extremes.

SCARY MATH

In the winter of 1997, scientists counted more than a billion monarchs in the Mexican forests. Now, that number is less than 36 million. Monarchs used to spread over 44 acres of land in Mexico's fir forests. Now, the area is less than two acres.

CLIMATE CHANGE

Global climate change affects monarchs in many ways. Climate change leads to more extreme weather, which means more extreme storms. In 2002, seventy-five percent of the wintering monarch population in Mexico was killed by one storm.

Droughts are also bad for monarchs. They kill milkweed and the wildflowers that adult monarchs need for high-energy nectar. Many monarchs starved during the recent extreme droughts in the American Southwest.

Monarchs need consistent cold "triggers" as cues to move south to Mexico for the winter. Climate change has made weather patterns more irregular, and monarchs get confused. When the weather warms in places where it's usually cold, monarchs sometimes fly north instead of south, ending up in places where it's too cold for them to live. If weather conditions are dry, monarchs can survive below-freezing temperatures. But if the weather is wet and the temperature drops, they freeze. As the climate warms up, more monarchs have been killed by a microscopic parasite that thrives in warmer weather.

The monarch's decline has a circular effect. Biologists believe that chemical cues left behind by one year's migrating monarchs give the next year's migrators a trail to follow. If not enough butterflies leave a scent, the chemical signals may not be strong enough for the next generation to follow.

All of this is bad for monarchs, but it's also bad for the bird, mouse, and spider species that can tolerate the monarch's milkweed toxins and prey on them. The monarch's decline also causes problems for people who live near the monarch groves in Mexico and depend on income from tourists who come to see the monarchs.

Droughts can damage habitats and the wildlife that live in them.

ROADSIDE ASSISTANCE

To protect the monarchs, the Mexican government created the Monarch Butterfly Biosphere Reserve. The Reserve now protects 217 square miles of forests in the Sierra Madre. In this area, no logging can take place, so the butterfly's habitat can be preserved.

In the United States, there are programs that teach people how to plant butterfly gardens to help monarchs. Monarch Watch has a program called the Monarch Waystations (monarchwatch.org/waystations). A waystation is a place where milkweed is planted to attract monarchs. National Wildlife Federation's Garden for Wildlife program (nwf.org/garden) is another. There are thousands of monarch-friendly gardens in the United States now. You can even start one in your own backyard! Just plant milkweed seed for caterpillars and flowers that provide nectar to adults.

CATCHING UP WITH MONARCHS

The monarchs' wintering season begins in October, peaks in December, and ends by March. You can catch up with many clusters of monarchs in the late fall in central California. When they cluster, monarchs can look like dead leaves until the sun hits them and they start to flutter! Picture tens of thousands of butterflies on one tree, making a gentle swishing sound as their wings flutter. In many of the monarchs' wintering locations in the United States, the best time to see them is February.

- **Ellwood Main Monarch Grove, Goleta, California**
  goletabutterflygrove.com
  Up to 50,000 butterflies a year visit here. You can see them flutter most often in the early afternoon from December through February.

- **Coronado Butterfly Preserve, Goleta, California**
  sblandtrust.org/coronado-butterfly-preserve-2
  The largest preserve in California, this grove hosts the most butterflies between December and February.

- **Pismo Beach Monarch Butterfly Grove, Pismo Beach, California**
  monarchbutterfly.org
  One of the largest wintering populations in California is found here. Experts say the best time to see them is in the late morning and early afternoon through February.

- **Natural Bridges State Beach, Santa Cruz, California**
  parks.ca.gov/?page_id=541
  From November to mid-February, you can find monarchs here. The park even holds a migration festival in February.

- **Pacific Grove, California**
  Pacific Grove is known as Butterfly Town, U.S.A., because so many monarchs stop here for the winter. The best time to see them is in the early afternoon on sunny days.

FURTHER EXPLORING

Mystery Migrators

Mule deer are native to the North American West. They were named for their unusually large ears, which look a little bit like mule ears. Biologists had always thought that mule deer were non-migratory. Just a few years ago, though, new technology helped them discover that some mule deer migrate more than 150 miles each year, which is the longest land mammal migration in the United States.

Single File, Please!

The Florida spiny lobster is a warm-water lobster. The larvae hatch in shallow water, where their main predator, the lionfish, can't catch them. When they mature and autumn arrives, it's time to migrate to deeper water. To travel, spiny lobsters form groups of fifty to sixty. They line up in a row and migrate single-file, marching across the sea floor day and night for two days. The lobsters touch their antennae to the tail or legs of the lobster in front of them. Biologists believe traveling this way helps protect the lobsters and helps them to travel faster, as much as half a mile per day.

Blue Moves

Bluefish migration might just be a little too predictable for the species' own good. These fish live in the North American waters, spending the winter in Florida and migrating to northern waters in the late spring and early summer, traveling in big schools. Fishermen know exactly where to find them on their migration route, and they're one of the most popular catches for sport fishermen.

Geese on the Go

Snow geese (left and below left) get their name from the snowy color of their feathers and from the snowy places where they roost in the winter, including the tundra of Northern Canada and Alaska. Snow geese have one of the longest bird migration paths in North America, traveling as far as 3,000 miles. They travel in flocks of thousands, so you may see them migrating over the Midwest. It's a sight to see!

Canada geese (below) are one of North America's best-known migrators. These long-necked geese can be seen flying in V-shaped formations over every state in the lower 48 of the United States. Canada geese can fly up to 1,500 miles in a single day! In recent years, Canada geese have made news because instead of flying back to their northern homes in Canada in the spring, many have decided to stay in warmer climates in the United States, often making their homes on golf courses!

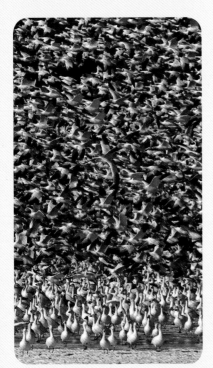

FURTHER EXPLORING

Research It Yourself!

Wildebeests, zebras, Asian elephants, and caribou have some of the world's most interesting migrations. Learn more by researching details of their migrations. How are they similar to the North American mammal migrations you read about in this book? How are they different?

Here are some good places to start your research adventure.

Massive Migrations, National Wildlife Federation
nwf.org/pdf/2011/Massive-Migrations-9to12.pdf

Endangered Migrations, National Wildlife Federation
nwf.org/news-and-magazines/national-wildlife/birds/archives/2010/endangered-migrations.aspx

Nature: Migration, British Broadcasting Corporation
bbc.co.uk/nature/adaptations/Animal_migration

Lemming Lore

Lemmings live in Arctic regions, including northern Alaska, Norway, and Sweden. They're tiny animals that migrate in very big groups when they sense their food source is running low. Often, their migration path crosses bodies of water, and many lemmings drown while crossing. These drownings led some people to believe that lemmings were trying to drown themselves on purpose, but that's a myth.

Sky Skimmers

Known for its incredibly thin, sharp bill that "skims" the water's surface in search of food, the skimmer is a sea bird found all over the Pacific and Atlantic coasts of North America. You can see them migrating in large groups along each coast in the spring and early fall.

Jelly Journeys

Jellyfish Lake is a very unusual lake on an island of Palau in the South Pacific Ocean. It connects to the ocean through tunnels, but the animal life developed separately from their ocean relatives. Every day, golden jellyfish migrate within the lake, moving with the sun to avoid shadows and get the nutrients they need from the water.

INDEX

INDEX

Keep exploring! Above: How are the migration paths of humpback whales different from gray whale migration paths? Above right: Viceroy butterflies mimic the wing patterns and colors of monarchs, which helps protect them from predators even though they're not toxic. Do viceroys migrate? Have questions about other wildlife species and their migration paths? Visit nwf.org/RangerRick and search "migration."

GLOSSARY

CARNIVORE: An animal that consumes other animals.

FLUKES: A whale's tail.

FLYWAY: A bird's or flying insect's migration path.

FORBS: Non-woody flowering plants such as sunflower, milkweed, or clover.

FRAGMENTATION: When a large habitat is broken up into smaller, noncontinuous areas, usually by human development or activity.

HERBIVORE: An animal that eats plants.

HERPTILE: A nickname for reptiles and amphibians together.

INCUBATE: In the case of eggs, to keep warm before hatching.

INVASIVE SPECIES: A species that is not local or native to an area that has been introduced by human activity and that causes great damage to its new ecosystem where it no longer has the same predators or habitat limits.

LARVA: The worm-like stage of many insects before they enter the adult stage of their lifecycle.

METABOLISM: The way a living creature's body uses food and water to grow and maintain life.

OMNIVORE: An animal that eats both plants and animals.

PREDATOR: An animal that hunts and feeds on other animals.

PREY: An animal hunted or eaten by another animal.

ROOST: To sleep (verb). A place where animals sleep (noun).

SAGEBRUSH: A shrub that lives in the dry desert areas of western North America.

SAVANNA: A grassy plain usually found in sub-tropical regions.

SEMI-DORMANT: Not quite hibernation, but a state of being in which animals conserve energy.

SPAWN: An egg deposit made by fish, frogs, mollusks, and other water-based animals.

SPECIES: A group of organisms that have common traits and can produce young.

TOXIN: A poisonous substance.

VERNAL POOLS: Temporary bodies of water that appear in the spring when snow and ice melts and after winter and spring rains.

CREDITS

PHOTOGRAPHY AND ILLUSTRATIONS

FROM THE PHOTOGRAPHY ARCHIVES OF THE NATIONAL WILDLIFE FEDERATION:

Christine Bloor, Deidre Brown, Howard Cheek, Phoebe Clark, Shelley Ellis, Robert Esbensen, Charles Gonzalez, Skip Hall, Danny Hancock, Deidre Heindl, Martha Hitchiner, John Hobbs, Robyn Hoffenberg, John Hoffman, Tamie Hopp, Brett Klaproth, Martin Knippel, Panagiotis Laskarakis, Eric C. Lefranc, David Lowenstern, Shellie Martyn, Casey McCurdy, Michael McKinne, Christina Parrott, Vicki Peterson, Lois Pflueger, Robert Rashkow, Kelli Reed, George Ritchey, Sarah Rose, Kenneth Schwartz, Lois Settlemeyer, Robert Strickland, Kiat Choon Teo, Laura J. Vosejpka, Pamela Wanamaker, Chad Watts, Paul Whitten, Lydia Williams, Marijka Willis, and Teri Zambon

FROM SHUTTERSTOCK:

Solodov Alexey, Greg Amptman, AndreAnita, Tobias Arhelger, Sekar B, Jeffrey B. Banke, Thomas Barrat, BMJ, Steve Bower, Paul Brennan, Kipling Brock, Jennifer Nicole Buchanan, Cameilia, Tony Campbell, Canadapanda, Ann Cantelow, Chameleons Eye, Creation, Jo Crebbin, Cubm, Ethan Daniels, Dennis W. Donohue, James Michael Dorsey, Jace Duval, Feel4nature, Dean Fikar, Stephen Finn, Svetlana Foote, Freesoulproduction, Bildagentur Zoonar Gmbh, Tom Grundy, Arto Hakola, Jan-Dirk Hansen, Holbox, Rob Holdorp, Jiang Hongyan, Jean Huls, Eric Isselee, Ronald Wilfred Jansen, Shaun Jeffers, Josh92mac, JPS, Cathy Keifer, Kojihirano, Alan Kraft, Sergey Krasnoshchokov, Krasowit, Lasse Kristensen, Ksanawo, Leaves002, Lebendkulturen.de, Maksimilian, Maxmacs, Chris Moody, Ryan Morgan, NCG, Debbie Oetgen, Sari O'Neal, Oorka, Outdoorsman, Pictureguy, Pmphoto, Joy Prescott, Puttsk, Dmytro Pylypenko, Marcio Jose Bastos Silva, Alexander Raths, Tom Reichner, Jeremy Richards, Rigucci, Romarti, Ginger Livingston Sanders, Snap2Art, Jason Steel, Lorraine Swanson, Tristan Tan, TFoxFoto, Tania Thomson, Tntphototravis, Trouvik, Sergey Uryadnikov, Val_Iva, Verityjohnson, Michael Warwick, Welcomia, K. West, Christopher Wood, and Zizar

FROM OTHER SOURCES:

Bob Armstrong, Chad Deaton/USDA Forest Service/Shawnee National Forest, Tom Lynn, Lauren Medford, wNOAA/NMFS/NWFSC/FED/PF, and Benjamin Sandford

CREDITS

RESEARCH

AUTHORS/EXPERTS CONSULTED:

Joel Berger, Kim Berger, Richard Conniff, Mary Dalheim, Terry Gamppar, Daniel Glick, Susan Goldenberg, Alex Hawes, Lisa Huchins, Brian Maffly, Shannon Miller, David Mizejewski, Keith Morelli, Sophia Rosenbaum, Philip Ross, Chip Taylor, Anne Thompson, Jeff Tollefson, Louise Wagenknecht, and Powell Wheeler

WEBSITES CONSULTED:

Defenders of Wildlife, defenders.org

Grand Teton National Park, nps.gov/grte/index.htm

International Crane Foundation, savingcranes.org/

The Marine Mammal Center, marinemammalcenter.org

Monarch Watch, monarchwatch.org/tagmig/index.htm

National Wildlife Federation, nwf.org and nwf.org/RangerRick

Nebraska Flyway, nebraskaflyway.com

The Ocean Institute, ocean-institute.org

The Oceanic Society, oceanicsociety.org

Pacific Salmon Commission, psc.org

Point Reyes National Seashore, nps.gov/pore/planyourvisit/wildlife_viewing_whales.htm

Polar Bears International, polarbearsinternational.org

The Rowe Sanctuary, National Audubon Society, rowe.audubon.org

Save the Manatee, savethemanatee.org

Sirenia Project, fl.biology.usgs.gov/Manatees/manatees.html

Shawnee National Forest, fs.usda.gov/shawnee

Think Salmon, thinksalmon.com

U.S. Fish and Wildlife Service, fws.gov

Wildlife Conservation Society, wcsnorthamerica.org

Yellowstone National Park, nps.gov/yell/index.htm